# A Soldier's Life

## Simon Rose

Weigl

Published by Weigl Educational Publishers Limited
6325 – 10 Street SE
Calgary, Alberta, Canada
T2H 2Z9

Website: www.weigl.ca

Library and Archives Canada Cataloguing in Publication

Rose, Simon, 1961-, author
    A soldier's life / Simon Rose.

(Canada in World War I)
Includes index.
Issued in print and electronic formats.
ISBN 978-1-77071-246-1 (bound).--ISBN 978-1-77071-247-8 (pbk.).--
ISBN 978-1-77071-248-5 (epub)

    1. World War, 1914-1918--Juvenile literature.  2. World War,
1914-1918--Canada--Juvenile literature.  3. Canada--History--
1914-1918--Juvenile literature.  I. Title.

D522.7.R68 2013              j940.3'71          C2013-904317-9
                                                C2013-904318-7

Printed in the United States of America
1 2 3 4 5 6 7 8 9 0  17 16 15 14 13

072013
WEP130613

We acknowledge the financial support of the Government of Canada
through the Canada Book Fund for our publishing activities.

Photograph and Text Credits
Alamy: pages 4, 8, 9, 13; Canada's War Museum: pages 12, 13; Getty
Images: pages 4, 5, 6, 8, 9, 10, 11, 13; iStockphoto: page 9; Trent
University Archives: page 22 (Helen Fowlds)

Every reasonable effort has been made to trace ownership and to obtain
permission to reprint copyright material. The publishers would be
pleased to have any errors or omissions brought to their attention so
that they may be corrected in subsequent printings.

Senior Editor
Aaron Carr

Art Director
Terry Paulhus

# A Soldier's Life

## CONTENTS

At the start of the war, tanks were of limited value. They were easily stopped by enemy fire and rough terrain.

Horses were an important part of most armies during World War I.

Most Canadian soldiers fought from trenches after the war's progress slowed down in December 1914.

Charging from the trenches was one of a soldier's most terrifying moments.

# The War Begins

Many men joined the armed forces from a sense of loyalty to their country and the empire.

Great Britain declared war on Germany on August 4, 1914. As a member of the British Empire, Canada was automatically at war as well. As a separate British **colony**, Newfoundland was also at war. At that time, many Canadians had very strong ties to Great Britain. People marched and sang in the streets to show their support for the war effort.

Canada was a self-governing **dominion**, but the government had offered to supply troops if Great Britain went to war. When the fighting began, Canada only had about 3,000 men serving in its armed forces. There were also a number of **militia** units in different parts of Canada. Despite this, Canada promised to send 25,000 soldiers overseas to create a Canadian **division**.

In August 1914, it was decided to create the **Canadian Expeditionary Force (CEF)**. Recruiting offices opened across the country, and men enlisted in great numbers. Very soon, almost 40,000 men had joined the armed forces. About 70 percent of these soldiers were born in Great Britain, although many had lived in Canada for years and considered themselves Canadians. During the course of the war, the number of Canadian-born soldiers increased. By 1918, more than half of all CEF soldiers had been born in Canada.

At the beginning of the war, soldiers had to be at least 1.6 metres tall and have good eyesight, healthy teeth, and arched feet. They also had to be between 18 and 45 years of age. As a result, many volunteers were turned away. Military recruiters also rejected most minorities early in the war. On October 3, 1914, the first Canadian soldiers set sail for Great Britain. By December, the first Canadian units were on the **front line** in France.

# Theatre of War

**M**ost of the soldiers and airmen from Canada and Newfoundland fought in northern France and Belgium. The Newfoundland **Regiment** also fought in Turkey, where it was almost wiped out in the 1915 Gallipoli campaign. Canadian nurses were stationed in France but also served in the eastern Mediterranean. Canadian military and civilian sailors served on ships taking supplies to Great Britain and transporting troops both during and after the war.

Canadian soldiers fought in many of the major battles in World War I, sometimes playing a crucial role. **Allied** commanders often sent in the Canadians to help turn the tide if it appeared the Germans might win a battle. Canadian soldiers were respected as brave and effective soldiers and seen as an elite fighting force, even by the enemy. British Prime Minister David Lloyd George commented, "Whenever the Germans found the Canadian Corps coming into the line they prepared for the worst."

## Allied and German Forces on the Western Front

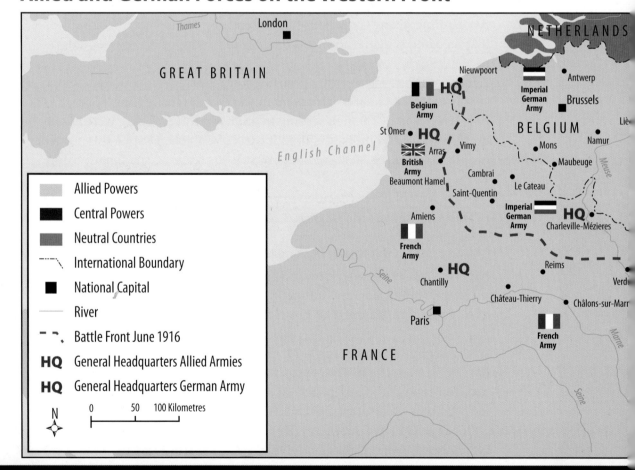

Like other soldiers on both sides of the war, Canadian troops faced new weapons on the battlefield, such as machine guns. They were also among the first Allied soldiers to be attacked by German poison gas. This occurred at the Second Battle of Ypres in 1915. Soldiers on the Western Front experienced **trench warfare** for much of the conflict. The opposing armies were mobile when the war began in August 1914, but the German attack soon stalled. Both sides dug trenches, which could be as close as 30 metres apart in some places. They fortified their positions with barbed wire, machine guns, and heavy **artillery**. The trenches stretched across parts of Belgium and northern and eastern France for almost 1,000 kilometres in what was called the Western Front.

Canadian soldiers manned trenches close to British positions along the Western Front. The areas between the Allied and German trenches were called "no man's land." These areas were the scene of some of the bloodiest fighting in the war. When an attack was launched, soldiers climbed out their trenches and tried to advance toward the enemy. They would then come under heavy enemy fire in no man's land, where there was often no cover to hide behind for protection. The number of battle casualties was usually very high, and attacks often resulted in failure. Even attacks that were considered successful often only involved an advance of a few metres, with many soldiers killed or wounded.

### The Canadian Soldier

The average age of Canadian soldiers in World War I was 26. Though age restrictions should have limited the number of people who could join the armed forces, thousands of both older and younger men lied about their age in order to enlist. The youngest soldier was only 10 years old, and the oldest was 80.

Canadian soldiers came from all parts of the country. In 1914, more Canadians lived in rural areas than in cities, but recruitment statistics only indicate where they enlisted, not where they lived. Ontario and the western provinces contributed the most troops, while fewer soldiers came from Quebec and the **Maritimes**.

Eighty percent of soldiers were unmarried. Most soldiers were literate, though many would not have been in school after grade six. Before joining the military, the majority of soldiers had worked as farmers or labourers. Even after **conscription** was introduced in 1917, most Canadian soldiers were still volunteers.

"THE PATH OF DUTY IS THE PATH TO GLORY."

**June 28** - Archduke Franz Ferdinand, heir to the throne of Austria-Hungary, is assassinated in Sarajevo.

**August 3** - Germany invades Belgium.

**August 4** - Great Britain declares war on Germany. Canada and Newfoundland are members of the British Empire and are now at war as well.

**October 3** - The first members of the CEF sail for Great Britain. They arrive on October 14.

**December 21** - The first Canadian unit, Princess Patricia's Canadian Light **Infantry**, arrives in France.

**April 22 to 25** - The Second Battle of Ypres is the first major battle involving Canadian troops. After the battle, Francis Pegahmagabow is awarded the Military Medal.

**April 25** - The Gallipoli Campaign is launched by the Allies against Turkey in the eastern Mediterranean.

**October 21** - The Allies launch the Salonika Campaign in northern Greece, which finally ends in September 1918.

**December 8** - John McCrae's poem "In Flanders Fields" is first published by *Punch* magazine in London, England.

**January 9** - The Gallipoli Campaign ends in defeat for the Allies.

**July 1 to November 18** - Soldiers from Canada and Newfoundland are involved in the Battle of the Somme.

Though it became known as the war to end all wars, most world leaders believed the war would be very short with little destruction.

**March 3** - Helen Fowlds is awarded the Royal Red Cross (2nd Class) in a ceremony at Buckingham Palace in London, England. This award is for exceptional services in military nursing.

**April 9 to 12** - The Battle of Vimy Ridge takes place, ending with the victory of Canadian soldiers over the Germans.

**October 26 to November 10** - Canadian forces suffer more than 16,000 casualties in the Battle of Passchendaele.

**January 28** - John McCrae, the author of "In Flanders Fields," dies at age 45.

**June 27** - A German submarine, called a U-boat, torpedoes the Canadian hospital ship *Llandovery Castle*, killing 234 people.

**August 8 to November 11** - Canadian troops fight in many battles during the Hundred Days Offensive.

**October 4** - After showing great bravery in battle, Thomas Ricketts becomes the youngest soldier ever awarded the Victoria Cross.

**November 11** - George Price of the 28th **Battalion** is one of the last soldiers to die. He dies two minutes before the war officially ends when the **armistice** begins at 11 a.m.

Canadian soldiers saw some of the hardest fighting during the war since they were often sent into difficult situations because of their reputation for bravery.

# Training for War

Not long after recruitment offices opened across Canada, the armed forces swelled in numbers. However, the new soldiers needed to be trained before they could be sent to join the fighting in Europe. The main training base for Canadian soldiers in 1914 was at Valcartier, Quebec. A camp was quickly built at the base when war broke out. The camp eventually housed more than 35,000 troops. The new soldiers had very little time to learn how to use their weapons and equipment. The war was already raging in Europe, and Canadian troops were needed on the front line. In early October, the first 30,000 Canadian troops, along with soldiers from Newfoundland, sailed to Great Britain.

The soldiers arrived in Plymouth in mid-October and then travelled by train to the military training base at Salisbury Plain in southern England. The Canadians trained there for up to four months. A rainy winter in the area meant the soldiers trained in muddy conditions. They coped with the bad weather, but Canadian equipment was not suitable for the conditions and was soon exchanged for British equipment.

The Canadian soldiers had been recruited quickly and learned battlefield basics in Canada and Great Britain. However, their real training would begin once they were deployed on the front line. The first Canadian units arrived in France in December 1914, where they would soon engage the enemy in battle.

At first, there were no Canadian generals who were qualified to command the Canadian troops. Lieutenant-General E.A.H. Alderson was an experienced British officer who had previously commanded Canadian soldiers in the South African War. He led the 1st Canadian Division and later served as the first commander of the Canadian Corps from September 1915 until May 1916.

### Sir Arthur Currie

In 1917, Sir Arthur Currie became the first Canadian ever to lead the Canadian army. Currie trained the Canadians for some of their hardest fights, such as Vimy Ridge.

At Valcartier, soldiers learned how to handle their weapons, as well as basic tactics.

Once in Britain, Canadian soldiers trained more on Salisbury Plain.

Recruitment posters became an important way to get men to join the army.

General Alderson was replaced in 1916.

Many Canadian horses were also sent to Europe for use in the cavalry.

Cavalry training involved learning to fight with swords on horseback.

# World War I Uniforms

Soldiers wore a standard uniform when they were serving in the field. They also carried a kit that contained all the equipment they might need when spending time away from camp. A soldier always carried his gear with him when stationed on the front line.

## Helmet

The first Canadian soldiers sent to Europe wore a soft cap. After several men suffered head injuries from flying **shrapnel**, soldiers were issued steel helmets. These provided greater protection and weighed about 1 kilogram. A helmet protected soldiers from shrapnel injuries, but it did not stop bullets. A bullet could penetrate the metal helmet.

## Trousers

Like the tunic, a soldier's trousers were green-brown in colour and made from wool. Wrappings called puttees were worn over the lower legs of the trousers. The puttees provided the legs with protection and support.

## Boots

The boots worn by Canadian soldiers at the beginning of the war proved not to be strong enough to withstand the harsh conditions on the front line. The soles of the boots had a tendency to dissolve in the wet and muddy conditions of the trenches. As a result, Canadian soldiers began wearing British boots instead.

## Tunic

Uniforms had a tunic that soldiers wore as a jacket. The tunics were green-brown in colour and made from wool. The arm of the tunic featured a badge indicating the soldier's regiment. The colour of the shoulder straps varied. For infantry soldiers, the strap was dark blue, while soldiers serving in the artillery wore a red strap. In rifle battalions, the strap was green. For members of the cavalry, it was yellow.

### Gas Mask

Canadian soldiers in World War I used two different types of gas masks. The PH helmet was made of flannel and covered the soldier's entire head. The helmet had glass eyeholes and a metal tube so that the soldier could breathe through his mouth. To help counter the effects of a gas attack, the helmet was treated with protective chemicals. Later in the war, the PH helmet was replaced by the box respirator gas mask. This type of gas mask had an attached box containing chemicals that acted as a filter to remove poisons from the air the soldier was breathing. The box was carried in a bag on the soldier's chest, while the mask was strapped to his head.

### Webbing

Soldiers had a number of belts, harnesses, pouches, and straps that they wore over their uniforms. Known as webbing, these pieces of equipment were used to carry ammunition, cooking supplies, first aid kits, and even materials needed to build a small tent.

### Mess kit

Soldiers used mess kits to prepare and serve their food. The mess kit was one piece of equipment, but it could be separated into a food tray and a skillet. When not being used, the kit was attached to the soldier's webbing with his other equipment.

### Canteen

Human remains and war debris often contaminated the water near battlefields. The water was not usually safe to drink, so each soldier carried a water bottle strapped over his shoulder. It was very important that soldiers kept their canteens full in order to avoid dehydration.

### Pilots

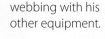

Pilots wore leather flying helmets, goggles, scarves, and leather overcoats. The padded helmet and coat were essential in the open cockpit, since it was very cold high up in the air above the battlefield. The scarf helped to prevent chafing on the neck, since the pilot would constantly swivel his head, scanning the sky for the enemy. The cold-weather flight suit had goggles and a face mask for winter flights, but pilots were also in danger of frostbite at higher altitudes.

# The War on the Ground

**M**ost Canadian soldiers served as ground forces in the infantry. These soldiers normally fight the enemy face to face, but this was not always the case in World War I.

In the fall of 1914, both sides dug long lines of trenches that were manned by infantry soldiers. They spent hours in the trenches in all kinds of weather, firing at the enemy positions or preparing for a possible attack. On the Western Front, trenches were typically between 90 and 275 metres apart. At Vimy Ridge, however, the distance was only 27 metres. To launch attacks, soldiers had to clamber out of their trenches and enter no man's land. There, they faced enemy machine gun and shellfire, which often led to heavy casualties.

Trench life could be very boring. It was also stressful. At times, it was even terrifying. Soldiers usually got very little sleep, which affected their mental and physical health. The waste created by the armies attracted rats, which spread disease. Lice caused trench fever, which gave the soldiers headaches and fevers. The cold, damp, and unsanitary conditions also led to a frostbite-like condition called trench foot, which could be very serious. Soldiers faced the constant threat of death from shells or **snipers**. Troops were also attacked with poison gas, which caused terrible injuries and death. Canadian soldiers on the Western Front were killed or wounded every day.

Soldiers were on constant guard against shell attacks from the enemy.

Enemy attacks often began at dawn. Each morning, infantry soldiers were instructed to "stand-to," which meant they had to be ready to guard the trench. If everything was quiet, it would be time for inspections and breakfast. The men then had chores, such as filling sandbags, making any necessary repairs, or cleaning latrines, or toilets. They worked below ground level in the daytime to avoid enemy snipers. At night, some soldiers would go into no man's land to repair barbed wire or dig a new trench. Raids on the enemy also took place under cover of darkness. These involved killing or capturing enemy soldiers or gathering **intelligence**.

"It was really a miserable day, quite miserable. We were lying practically on the bed of the river which had been shelled all to pieces and it was just a marshy bog … Our company headquarters got blown to pieces … before we started off … and the battle hadn't even begun."

*Alex Strachan, 43rd Battalion, Battle of Passchendaele, 1917*

Soldiers were also rotated to give them a break from the trenches. Soldiers usually served between four and six days at the front line and then spent an equal amount of time in the safer areas at the rear. Sometimes, soldiers were granted leave, or permission to go away from the fighting for a period of time.

When they had a break, soldiers often read, wrote letters, or played cards to pass the time.

# The War at Sea

The HMCS *Niobe* was given to Canada by Great Britain. It became the first ship of Canada's navy.

At the beginning of the war, Canada's navy only had about 350 sailors and two old ships, the HMCS *Niobe* and HMCS *Rainbow*. The Canadian Navy expanded during the war, but more than 3,000 Canadians served in the British Royal Navy from 1914 to 1918. The Royal Navy had previously protected Canada's coasts. Once the war began, however, the British were busy fighting the Germans closer to home. Canada had to defend itself. Despite its small size, the navy played a part in Canada's war effort.

The Canadian Navy kept track of vessels in local ports and those entering Canadian waters. If necessary, sailors inspected the ships' cargo. Sailors on smaller vessels patrolled the Atlantic coast searching for German U-boats and other signs of enemy activity. Some sailors worked on minesweepers. These small, wooden-hulled boats were used to find or destroy mines placed by U-boats in shipping lanes or at harbour entrances. The Canadian Navy also worked on intelligence gathering for the Allied cause. Sailors intercepted enemy messages and gave the information to the British.

During the war, U-boats sank thousands of Allied ships.

In addition to the navy, the government founded the Merchant Marine in early 1918. Civilian sailors served on ships taking supplies on dangerous voyages across the Atlantic. Sailors spent much of their time at sea and were in constant danger of attacks from German U-boats. As the war progressed, merchant ships began sailing in groups, called convoys, which were escorted by warships. Convoys were harder for U-boats to attack, but ships were still sunk. Although the exact number of casualties is not known, the experiences of Canadian civilian sailors later proved invaluable during World War II.

> "Heavy sea running—following a zig zag course … Still in danger zone, followed by torpedo (boat) destroyers who fired two shots at a German submarine supposed to have been seen. Tremendous excitement."
>
> *Colonel Edouard Leprohon, Canadian Senior Medical officer onboard the RMS Olympic, March 1918.*

The RMS *Olympic*, a sister vessel to the *Titanic*, was used as a **troop ship** during World War I. The *Olympic* transported Canadian soldiers across the Atlantic Ocean and took many of them home again when the war was over. At the height of the war, the ship faced great danger from German U-boats and had to keep changing course to avoid detection.

Germany had 38 U-boats by the time the war had broken out.

# The War in the Air

Aircraft were widely used in combat for the first time during World War I. Canada did not have its own air force until the final months of the war, yet more than 23,000 Canadians served with British flying services. This included pilots as well as aircrew, who maintained and repaired aircraft. The Royal Flying Corps set up training schools in southern Ontario and regularly recruited Canadian pilots.

Planes were constantly being lost in battle, so new planes were always being built to replace those that had been shot down.

In the early months of the war, planes were used for **reconnaissance** and intelligence gathering. Their flights took them over hostile territory so they could observe the positions of enemy ground and naval forces. Their reports helped commanders plan their battle strategies. Pilots often had to fly low and reduce their speed to photograph forces on the ground. This made them easier targets for enemy fighters and anti-aircraft guns. Some planes were built as two-seaters, with the person in the rear operating a machine gun.

There was never a shortage of volunteers to join the air force. Canadian army soldiers sometimes tried to get transferred to the air force to escape life in the trenches. Those who had mechanical skills worked as aircrew. In aerial combat, pilots took part in what were known as dogfights. Opposing aircraft would dive or fly at each other with their machine guns firing, trying to shoot down the enemy plane.

"In nearly all cases where machines have been downed, it was during a fight which had been very short, and the successful burst of fire had occurred within the space of a minute after the beginning of actual hostilities."

*Lieutenant Colonel Billy Bishop, Canadian air ace with the British Royal Air Force*

In World War I, there were 171 Canadian air aces. These were pilots or gunners who had shot down five or more enemy aircraft or airships. Air aces included Billy Bishop, with 72 kills, Raymond Collishaw, with 60, and William G. Barker, with 50. Canadian fliers received almost 500 British decorations for bravery between 1914 and 1918.

Although pilots were sometimes called "Knights of the Sky," the war in the air was cruel and deadly. Very few men survived if their plane caught fire or if they were wounded in the air. Only a small number of pilots successfully got out of their planes, and crash landings often led to serious injury or even death.

The life expectancy of a new pilot was only a few weeks.

Planes were not considered to be a valuable weapon until after the war had started.

# Nurses at War

More than 3,000 nurses served in the Canadian Army Medical Corps (CAMC) during World War I. Canada's Nursing Sisters wore blue uniforms and white veils and were nicknamed "bluebirds" by the soldiers they helped. Canadian military nurses were all women between the ages of 21 and 38 who had been trained as nurses before the outbreak of the war. All of the nurses were volunteers, and they served in France and the eastern Mediterranean.

Medical units were initially established in hospitals far from the battlefields. Later, casualty clearing stations were set up close to the front line to provide quicker and more effective care for those soldiers who were injured. Ambulances brought the wounded to the stations. Wounds were cleaned and treated if possible, but soldiers with severe wounds were often sent to hospitals farther away from the fighting.

The early assessment and treatment possible at the stations helped medical staff to deal with the number of casualties and the many different types of battle injuries. Nurses assisted the doctors and were often responsible for cleaning and caring for wounds. This was very important to prevent soldiers from dying from a secondary infection. However, the stations were very close to the front line and exposed the nurses to great danger. The advance areas were often hit by shellfire or attacked during air raids.

Canadian nurses often had to drive ambulances into the war zone to pick up the wounded.

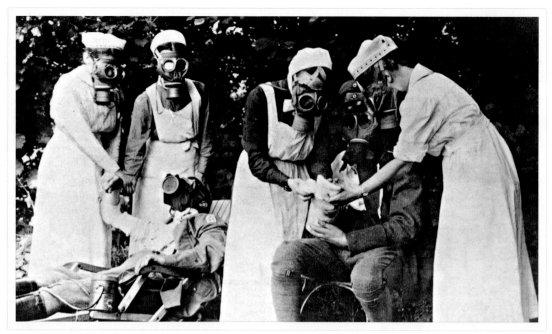

Nurses on both sides of the war had to deal with such dangers as poison gas attacks.

The stations where nurses worked presented other challenges as well. The camps sometimes contained only tents or poorly built shacks. The sheer number of wounded and limited supplies often meant that nurses tended to soldiers who were lying on the ground. Stationary hospitals had better conditions. In these hospitals, the wounded received better care, and they could better recover from their injuries. Yet many of these hospitals were little more than huts that could be moved quickly from one place to another if necessary. The nurses had an exhausting workload and worked in primitive conditions. There were no **antibiotics** during World War I, and the number of wounded frequently increased due to outbreaks of disease. Nurses often had to deal with rats and fleas at the casualty clearing stations. In areas such as the Mediterranean, nurses also faced extremes of temperature.

Nurses did not just face danger on land. They also cared for wounded soldiers on hospital ships. On June 27, 1918, a German U-boat torpedoed the Canadian hospital ship, HMHS *Llandovery Castle*, off the southern coast of Ireland. The sinking left 234 people dead, including 14 nurses. In total, 53 Canadian nurses lost their lives in the line of duty during World War I.

"Big convoy tonight. Many gassed and burned by 'liquid fire' shells. Some are very desperately injured, especially about the eyes. The new gas masks recently provided have proved inadequate, the gas penetrates and burns the mask."

*Alice Isaacson, Canadian Army Nursing Corps, July 17, 1917*

# Heroic Canadians

## William (Billy) Avery Bishop (1884–1956)

During World War I, Billy Bishop was the most successful fighter pilot in the British Empire's armed forces.

Bishop was born in Owen Sound, Ontario. Bishop joined the CEF in 1914 as an infantry soldier. The next year, he requested a transfer to the British Royal Flying Corps. He qualified as a pilot in 1917. At the front line in France, Bishop quickly established himself as an ace. When he flew behind enemy lines on a dangerous mission and shot down three German planes, he was awarded the Victoria Cross, Great Britain's highest award for bravery in combat. From 1917 to 1918, Bishop shot down 72 enemy planes. In June 1918, Bishop was transferred to England, where he created a Canadian flying squadron.

In 1938, Bishop was appointed honorary air marshal of the Royal Canadian Air Force. He later helped with recruitment during World War II.

## John McCrae (1872–1918)

John McCrae was the author of "In Flanders Fields," which became one of the most well-known poems of World War I. This poem is often read at Remembrance Day ceremonies across Canada.

McCrae was born in Guelph, Ontario. He graduated with a medical degree from the University of Toronto in 1898 and served as a lieutenant in the Royal Canadian Artillery in the South African War. In 1914, McCrae became a major and brigade surgeon with the 1st Brigade, Canadian Field Artillery, in the CEF.

McCrae's brigade was part of the Second Battle of Ypres and was attacked by the Germans using chlorine gas. More than half of the brigade was killed in the battle. McCrae wrote "In Flanders Fields" while waiting for wounded soldiers to arrive for treatment. The poem was first published in *Punch* magazine in London, England, in December 1915.

## Thomas Ricketts (1901–1967)

Thomas Ricketts was the youngest soldier ever to be awarded the Victoria Cross.

In 1916, Ricketts lied about his age and joined the Royal Newfoundland Regiment. On October 14, 1918, his unit was pinned down by German fire. Ricketts volunteered to flank the German position. Against heavy enemy fire, Ricketts and his fellow soldiers got within 275 metres of the Germans but ran out of ammunition. The only choices were to retreat or go back for more bullets.

His Victoria Cross citation states, "Private Ricketts at once realized the situation. He doubled back 100 yards, procured some ammunition and dashed back to the Lewis gun, and by very accurate fire drove the enemy and their gun teams into a farm. His platoon then advanced without casualties, and captured four field guns, four machine guns and eight prisoners." Ricketts was only 17 years old.

### Francis Pegahmagabow (1891–1952)

Francis Pegahmagabow was the most **decorated** of any Aboriginal Canadian in World War I. He was the war's most successful sniper, killing 378 Germans and capturing 300.

Pegahmagabow was an Ojibwa from the Parry Island Band in Ontario. He volunteered for the CEF and was assigned to the 1st Canadian Infantry Battalion. He was involved in the Second Battle of Ypres. After the battle, He was awarded the Military Medal for bravery under fire.

Pegahmagabow was wounded at the Battle of the Somme, and he received a second commendation at the Battle of Passchendaele. He received a third commendation after the Battle of the Scarpe in 1918.

Pegahmagabow later became chief of the Parry Island Band. In 1943, he became supreme chief of the Native Independent Government.

### Helen Fowlds (1889–1965)

Helen Fowlds was one of more than 2,500 Canadian nurses who served overseas in World War I. Her letters home to Canada are a valuable historical resource and provide many firsthand accounts of events during the conflict.

Fowlds was born in Hastings, Ontario. When the war began, Fowlds enlisted as a nurse and later sailed to Great Britain with other nurses from Toronto and Montreal as part of the Canadian Army Medical Corp. They arrived in France in March 1915.

Fowlds worked in the eastern Mediterranean and Egypt. In 1916, however, she suffered from a respiratory infection and left for Great Britain. In March 1917, she was awarded the Royal Red Cross (second class) for her wartime services. She died in 1965, and her letters, diaries, and papers were given to Trent University in Ontario.

### Georges Vanier (1888–1967)

Georges Vanier was a founding member of the 22nd Battalion of the Canadian Expeditionary Force and a decorated officer during World War I.

Vanier was born in Montreal, Quebec. After graduating from university, he became a lawyer. He enlisted in the armed forces shortly after the war began. Vanier helped create the 22nd Battalion, Canada's first French-Canadian volunteer unit. He served with the battalion as an officer and, for a short time, its commander. In Europe, Vanier fought in several battles. He was awarded the Military Cross for bravery in 1916. In 1918, Vanier was shot in the chest and legs while leading an attack at Chérisy, France. For his bravery and effort, he received a second Military Cross and a Distinguished Service Order.

Vanier became Canada's first French-Canadian governor general in 1959.

# Canada's War

Canadians served in many different areas during World War I. Most of the fighting they were involved in took place in a small area of northern France and Belgium, but soldiers, airmen, sailors, and nurses also served in the eastern Mediterranean, on ships in the North Atlantic, and at ports and training facilities across Canada. Soldiers from Newfoundland were involved in the Gallipoli campaign in Turkey. Canadian nurses tended to wounded soldiers in all three branches of the military. They worked in a total of 30 hospitals and casualty clearing stations throughout Europe, in addition to those nurses who served at sea on hospital ships.

Many recruits were very young when they signed up to serve their country.

The first Canadian nurses sent overseas to treat the war wounded were members of religious orders. This is why they became known as Canada's Nursing Sisters.

# By the Numbers

World War I saw the largest mobilization of weapons and troops the world had ever known. During the war, new weapons were developed and used, including tanks and poison gas. By the end of the conflict more than 15 million people were dead.

## Former Occupations of Soldiers

| Occupation | Percentage |
| --- | --- |
| Agriculture | 19.8 |
| Manufacturing | 12.6 |
| Labourers | 12.3 |
| Transportation | 9.5 |
| Building trades | 9.3 |
| Clerical | 8.6 |
| Domestic and personal services | 5.1 |
| Professional | 4.8 |
| Mercantile | 3.7 |
| Students | 2.4 |
| Mining | 2.3 |
| Forestry | 1.9 |
| Engineers, firemen | 1.9 |
| Other | 1.4 |
| Mechanics | 1.1 |
| Printers, engravers | 1.0 |
| Civil and municipal | 1.0 |
| Unknown | 0.8 |
| Hunting and fishing | 0.7 |

*numbers do not add up to 100% due to rounding

Canadians suffered some of the highest casualties of Commonwealth countries.

## The Price of Victory

**595,000** enlisted

**418,000** served overseas

**35,666** killed in action

**12,420** died of wounds

**5,405** died of disease

**155,799** wounded

**3,575** prisoners of war

**4,671** presumed dead

**425** missing

**2,221** deaths in Canada

**60,383** total dead

# The War Comes to an End

The war ended on November 11, 1918, but it took time to send all of the Canadian soldiers home. Physical training programs, sports, and recreational activities kept the men occupied while they waited to travel back to Canada. The Khaki University, which was first established in 1917, offered the bored soldiers educational courses from elementary to university level. Eventually, about 50,000 Canadians were involved in the program, which helped prepare soldiers for their return to civilian life.

It was a challenge to get all of the soldiers back home quickly. Sometimes, there were not enough suitable ships available, and strikes by dock or railway workers in Great Britain led to delays. In Canada, there were only two large ice-free ports— Saint John, New Brunswick, and Halifax, Nova Scotia. At first, Canadian railroads also had difficulty handling the arrival of such large numbers of people. There were some disturbances by soldiers who were frustrated at the delays, but by August 1919, most Canadians had arrived at their homes.

The transition back to civilian life proved challenging for some people, especially those who had been away the longest. It was also difficult for the Canadian economy to support hundreds of thousands of returning veterans. Some soldiers were able to go back to their old jobs. Others were not so lucky. Once the war was over, companies that had been producing military supplies cut their workforce or even closed down. To make things a little easier for veterans, the government set up the Department of Soldiers' Civil Re-establishment in 1918 to give soldiers job training. However, a weak economy during 1919 and 1920 left many Canadians out of work, including veterans.

The armistice of November 11 was not an actual surrender by Germany. The final peace treaty to officially end the war would not be signed until 1919.

The government also established pension and benefit programs for those who had been wounded in the fighting. This caused some problems, however. Though former soldiers who had lost limbs in the war had few problems receiving benefits, other people were refused. Men suffering from the effects of gas or with emotional or mental problems often had difficulty proving that their conditions were war-related.

Many soldiers were not able to return home until 1919.

The armistice that ended the war was signed in a railway car in the forest of Compiègne at 5:10 a.m.

Some soldiers collected mementos, which they took home with them.

Canadian soldiers marched through the streets celebrating the end of the war.

# Preparing for Battle

Canadian forces in World War I gained a reputation as some of the bravest and most effective Allied soldiers on the Western Front. Using the Internet, books from your local library, and any other sources you can find, learn how a Canadian soldier prepared for a battle in World War I. Study a specific battle, such as Vimy Ridge.

- What kinds of preparations would you need to make the day before the battle?
- How would you spend the final hour before going into battle?
- What kinds of conditions were you likely to encounter, once you were on the battlefield?
- What kind of care could you expect if you were injured during the battle?
- What would you expect to happen if the enemy captured you?

Draw a concept web based on your findings, and use the concept web you created to help you write a report.

# Concept Web

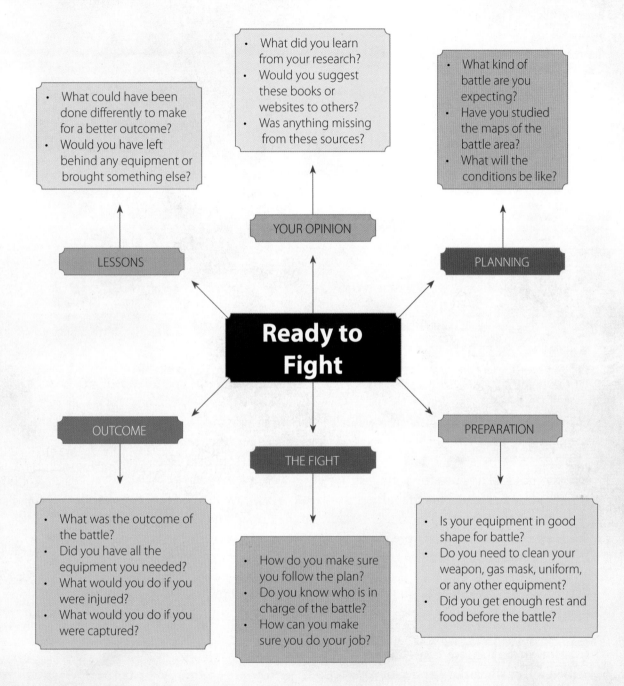

**What could have been done differently to make for a better outcome?**
- What could have been done differently to make for a better outcome?
- Would you have left behind any equipment or brought something else?

**YOUR OPINION**
- What did you learn from your research?
- Would you suggest these books or websites to others?
- Was anything missing from these sources?

**PLANNING**
- What kind of battle are you expecting?
- Have you studied the maps of the battle area?
- What will the conditions be like?

**LESSONS**

**Ready to Fight**

**OUTCOME**
- What was the outcome of the battle?
- Did you have all the equipment you needed?
- What would you do if you were injured?
- What would you do if you were captured?

**THE FIGHT**
- How do you make sure you follow the plan?
- Do you know who is in charge of the battle?
- How can you make sure you do your job?

**PREPARATION**
- Is your equipment in good shape for battle?
- Do you need to clean your weapon, gas mask, uniform, or any other equipment?
- Did you get enough rest and food before the battle?

# Test Your Knowledge

**1** Where were Canadian soldiers trained before being sent to Europe?

**2** Which Canadian hospital ship was sunk on June 27, 1918?

**3** Thomas Ricketts was the youngest soldier to be awarded what medal?

**4** How many enemy kills were made by air ace Raymond Collishaw?

**5** What nickname did the soldiers give to Canadian nurses?

**6** How many men were in Canada's armed forces when the war began in 1914?

**7** What was the average age of the Canadian soldier in World War I ?

**8** What was the name of the sister ship of the *Titanic* that was used to transport troops in World War I?

**9** Who served as the first commander of the Canadian Corps from September 1915 until May 1916?

**10** What were the belts, harnesses, pouches, and straps called that soldiers wore over their uniforms?

**Answer Key**
1. Valcartier, Quebec 2. HMHS *Llandovery Castle*
3. Victoria Cross 4. 60 5. Bluebirds 6. About
3,000 7. 26 8. The *Olympic* 9. Lieutenant-
General E.A.H. Alderson 10. Webbing

# Further Resources

**CHECK IT OUT!**

www.warmuseum.ca/cwm/
exhibitions/guerre/home-e.aspx

www.canadaatwar.ca/page43.html

www.thecanadianencyclopedia.
com/articles/first-world-war-wwi

http://canadasnavalmemorial.ca/
history/battles-and-conicts/world-
war-i-1914-1918

# Glossary

**Allied:** relating to the forces of Great Britain, France, and Russia, including all related territories and colonies; later including Italy (1915) and the United States (1917)

**antibiotics:** medicines that kill bacteria

**armistice:** agreement to stop a war

**artillery:** large-caliber weapons, such as cannons

**battalion:** a military unit made up of 300 to 1,200 soldiers; several battalions usually form a regiment or a brigade

**Canadian Expeditionary Force (CEF):** Canada's field forces in Europe

**colony:** a country or area under the control of another country

**conscription:** mandatory enrollment in the armed forces

**decorated:** awarded medals for bravery in the field or for service in the armed forces

**division:** a main administrative or tactical unit in an army

**dominion:** self-governing territory of an empire

**front line:** the location where enemy armies face each other in battle

**infantry:** soldiers who fight on foot

**intelligence:** military information about the enemy

**Maritimes:** provinces of New Brunswick, Nova Scotia, and Prince Edward Island

**militia:** a military force that only works part-time

**reconnaissance:** the process of obtaining information on the position and strength of enemy forces

**regiment:** a military unit made up of two or more battalions

**shrapnel:** fragments from artillery fire and explosive devices

**snipers:** soldiers who shoot at targets from a concealed area

**trench warfare:** battle in which opposing armies fight from fortified defences dug into the ground

**troop ship:** a vessel carrying soldiers to and from the theatre

# Index